BRUNO GMÜNDER ■ EDITION EUROS

BEL AMI
Photos of Lukas

BRUNO GMÜNDER

© 1997, Bruno Gmünder Verlag
PO Box 61 01 04
10837 Berlin
Germany
Phone: ++49 (30) 615 00 30

Photographs Copyright © 1997
Bel Ami ™, All rights reserved.
Lithography: Fotolitho Longo
Production & Layout:
Michael Taubenheim
Printing: Fotolitho Longo
Printed in Italy
ISBN 3-86187-111-4

Bisher sind in der Reihe EDITION EUROS erschienen:
(alle Bände sind im Format 15 x 19 cm mit Hardcover und haben 60 Seiten)

Nr 1: Clifford Baker
Druck in Duoton.
ISBN 3-86187-061-4
22.80 DM

Nr 2: Mark Brickell
Druck in Duoton.
ISBN 3-86187-062-2
22.80 DM

Nr 3: Benno Thoma
Druck in Duoton.
ISBN 3-86187-072-X
22.80 DM

Nr 4: Andrew Melick
Druck in Duoton.
ISBN 3-86187-073-8
22.80 DM

Nr 5: José Messana
Druck in Duoton.
ISBN 3-86187-074-6
22,80 DM

Nr 6: Desert Patrol, Photographs by Dook
80 Seiten, Druck in Duoton.
ISBN 3-86187-075-4
26.80 DM

Nr 7: Kingdome 19
Druck in Duoton.
ISBN 3-86187-089-4
22,80 DM

Nr 8: Bel Ami – Photos of Johan
Druck in Farbe
ISBN 3-86187-090-8
22.80 DM

Nr 9: Pedro Usabiaga
Druck in Duoton.
ISBN 3-86187-100-9
22.80 DM

Nr 10: Frank DiLeo
Druck in Duoton.
ISBN 3-86187-101-7
22,80 DM

Nr 11: Bel Ami – Photos of Lukas
Druck in Farbe
ISBN 3-86187-111-4
DM 22.80

EDITION EUROS

■ **BRUNO GMÜNDER**

Bruno Gmünder Verlag
Postfach 61 01 04
10921 Berlin